Baseball
Hall of Fame

by
Terry Janson Dunnahoo
and
Herma Silverstein

Crestwood House
New York

Maxwell Macmillan Canada
Toronto

Maxwell Macmillan International
New York   Oxford   Singapore   Sydney

Dedication
To my grandnephew Danny
TJD
To Leigh, my doubleheader ice-cream buddy
HS

Library of Congress Cataloging-in-Publication Data
Dunnahoo, Terry Janson.
Baseball Hall of Fame / by Terry Janson Dunnahoo and Herma Silverstein. — 1st ed.
p. cm. — (The Halls of fame)
Includes index.
Summary: Covers the history of baseball, its rules, great players, and memorable games as presented in the
Baseball Hall of Fame.
ISBN 0-89686-849-4
1. National Baseball Hall of Fame and Museum — History — Juvenile literature.
[1. Baseball — History. 2. National Baseball Hall of Fame and Museum.]
I. Silverstein, Herma. II.Title.
GV863.A1D85 1994   796.357'0973 — dc20   93-6915

Photo Credits
Photos on pages 15 (inset) and 18 courtesy of AP/Wide World Photos
All other photos/illustrations provided by the National Baseball Hall of Fame and Museum, Cooperstown, N.Y.
The publishers have made every effort to locate the copyright holders, but if they have overlooked any,
they will be pleased to make the necessary arrangements at the first opportunity.

Design
Tina Tarr Emmons

Layout and Production
Custom Communications

Crestwood House
Macmillan Publishing Company
866 Third Avenue
New York, NY 10022

Maxwell Macmillan Canada, Inc.
1200 Eglinton Avenue East
Suite 200
Don Mills, Ontario M3C 3N1

Macmillan Publishing Company is part of the Maxwell Communication Group of Companies.
First Edition
Printed in the United States of America
10 9 8 7 6 5 4 3 2 1

Table of Contents

According to legend, Abner Doubleday of Cooperstown, New York, invented baseball in 1839. Fans have loved the game ever since.

Chapter One

Take Me Out to the Ball Game:
The Birth of Baseball

How would you like to come face-to-face with Babe Ruth and Ted Williams? Or peek into Lou Gehrig's locker? Or see the nicks in the bat Willie Mays used when he hit four **home runs** in one game? You can. They're all on display in the Baseball Hall of Fame in Cooperstown, New York.

There might never have been a Baseball Hall of Fame if the United States and England hadn't been arguing over how baseball started. The English sided with British sportswriter Henry Chadwick, who wrote the first baseball rule book. Chadwick claimed that baseball came from the old English game of rounders. Like baseball, rounders was played with a bat and ball. The Americans sided with Albert G. Spalding, former Chicago White Stockings pitcher, who felt that baseball was an American game. Baseball was Spalding's favorite sport, and he didn't want to give anyone but Americans credit for inventing the game.

In 1905 the argument became so heated that Spalding created the Mills Commission, named after its chairman, A. G. Mills. Commission members asked people from all over the world to write to them if they had proof of where baseball began.

Letters poured in. But the one that caught the commission's attention was from Abner Graves, a former mining engineer, then in his 70s. Graves had lived in Cooperstown until he was a teenager. Then he ran away to join the California gold rush. He even rode for the pony express, then became a cattle rancher in Colorado. At 75 he married a 33-year-old woman. They didn't get along, and one of the issues they argued about was property. By the time he was 90, the arguments had become so heated that Graves got the crazy idea his wife was trying to poison him. So he shot her. Graves was sent to an insane asylum, where he stayed for the rest of his life.

Even though Graves's was an unstable character, the majority of the Mills Commission believed his letter saying that baseball was an American invention. In his letter Graves described the time he was shooting marbles with friends near a tailor shop in Cooperstown in 1839. According to Graves, another boy, Abner Doubleday, started telling them about a new game he had invented, which he called baseball.

Doubleday drew a diagram in the dirt and showed the boys where the bases would be. Doubleday's game had 11 players, including two short fielders and two catchers. Abner Graves and his friends couldn't wait to start playing the new game.

But they couldn't play by the tailor shop because an 1816 law said that "no person shall play at Ball in Second or West Streets in this village, under a penalty of $1, for each and every offense." So the boys raced to Elihu Phinney's cow pasture. Doubleday marked out a diamond-shaped field and gave each player a position.

The Mills Commission claimed that Abner Graves's letter was proof that baseball started in America, not in England. On December 30, 1907, the commission's report said that "the first scheme for playing baseball, according to the best evidence obtainable to date, was devised by Abner Doubleday, at Cooperstown, New York, in 1839."

Not everyone agreed with the commission. One reason was that there were two people named Abner Doubleday. They were cousins, and in 1839 both lived in Cooperstown. One was a 20-year-old West Point cadet, who later became a major general in the Civil War. The other was 10 years old and would live in Cooperstown most of his life.

At the time the Mills Commission did its work, both Abner Doubledays were dead. So nobody could ask them which one invented baseball. And the Mills Commission didn't bother to ask their families about the story, either.

During the early days of baseball, the Philadelphia Athletics and the Brooklyn Atlantics played the Second Great Match Game for the championship on October 22, 1866, in Philadelphia.

There was another reason why some people disagreed with the Mills Commission. At the time the older Doubleday was supposedly drawing the world's first baseball **diamond**, he hadn't finished his second year at West Point. And a West Point rule said cadets couldn't leave the academy until the end of their second year. So *that* Doubleday couldn't have been in Cooperstown in the summer of 1839.

Other people pointed out that the older Doubleday's diaries never mentioned baseball. And when he died in 1893, Doubleday's newspaper obituary said he was a man "who did not care for or go into outdoor sports."

Despite all the evidence against the first baseball game having been played in a cow pasture in Cooperstown, Spalding loved the legend. He was thrilled to believe the Mills Commission's statement that his favorite game was an American invention. But the Baseball Hall of Fame doesn't give credit for the invention of baseball to either of the Doubledays. Instead, it tells the story of the "myth" in its exhibits. The myth credits the Civil War hero Abner Doubleday as baseball's inventor.

The Hall of Fame's stand is that baseball evolved from earlier forms of stick and ball, which had been played since prehistory. According to the Hall of Fame, the game played today is based on the 1845 rule book of the New York Knickerbocker club. The club's rules were based on an American game called Town Ball, which was based on the British game of rounders.

In 1920 Cooperstown built a ballpark on what used to be Elihu Phinney's cow pasture. There the road to the Baseball Hall of Fame dead-ended until 1934. That year Abner Graves's possessions supposedly were discovered in a farmhouse in Fly Creek, New York, near Cooperstown. An old trunk had the "proof" that Graves's letter was right about baseball being an American invention. The proof was an old baseball — undersized, misshapen, and homemade. The ball cover had cracked open, and the cloth stuffing hung out.

Stephen Clark, a wealthy businessman and baseball fan, thought the ball was the one used by Abner Doubleday in the pasture. He bought the ball for $5 and named it the Abner Doubleday Baseball. Clark decided to display the ball in an exhibit to celebrate baseball's 100th anniversary in 1939. He asked his friend Alexander Cleland to look for other baseball souvenirs that could be displayed in the exhibit.

Begun as a museum, the Baseball Hall of Fame in Cooperstown, New York, was completed in 1939. It holds baseball souvenirs from all over the world and a library with every book ever written about the game.

Cleland found old uniforms, baseballs thrown by U.S. presidents, and bats belonging to famous players. So many people came to the exhibit that Cleland got the bright idea that would really put Cooperstown on the map — build a baseball museum. He also suggested that each year ten outstanding players should be honored in the museum.

Ford Frick, president of the National League, had even bigger ideas. He proposed that a Hall of Fame be built as part of the museum. As people heard about the Hall of Fame, baseball souvenirs poured in from all over the world. The Baseball Writers Association of America was chosen to nominate and elect players into the Hall of Fame. The first election was held in January 1936.

The winners were Ty Cobb, with 222 votes; Honus Wagner and Babe Ruth, each with 215; Christy Mathewson, with 205; and Walter Johnson, with 189. But the players weren't officially inducted into the Hall of Fame until June 12, 1939, after the building was finished. By that time 25 people had been elected. Eleven of them were still living.

These 11 were invited to Cooperstown for opening day ceremonies. They all came — except Ty Cobb. The baseball great, who could find his way around the bases blindfolded, couldn't find his way to Cooperstown. He got lost and was late arriving. That's why the first picture of the first Hall of Famers doesn't include the man who had a .367 lifetime **batting average**.

Since 1939 the Baseball Hall of Fame has expanded to hold its ever-growing collection, including a library containing every book ever written about baseball.

The original Doubleday Field is still on the spot where, according to the legend, Abner Doubleday drew his "diamond in the rough" in the cow pasture all those years ago. Whether Doubleday actually did or not, no one will ever know. One thing we do know. The 1816 ordinance against playing "at Ball" on the streets of Cooperstown does prove that boys played ball 23 years before Doubleday did or didn't invent baseball. Yet no one has proven that at the same time British boys weren't playing rounders.

No matter who really invented baseball, one thing is for sure. Baseball most likely started in an empty field where kids dreamed it would be fun to pick up a stick and hit a ball out of the pasture.

Chapter Two

Buy Me Some Peanuts and Cracker Jacks: The Game Grows

During the first year the Hall of Fame was open, 25,332 people paid 25 cents each to tour the Hall. Since then, millions of visitors have passed through its doors. So many souvenirs have been donated by baseball clubs, players, and fans that the Hall of Fame has become baseball's storage attic.

Almost every bat, ball, and glove that ever set a record is there. So are the shoes "Shoeless" Joe Jackson wore during the crooked 1919 Chicago White Sox **World Series**; the cap and ball Texas Rangers pitcher Nolan Ryan used when he pitched his record-breaking seventh no-hitter in 1991; and Babe Ruth's locker, complete with his bowling ball and shaving mug. Looking at his locker, you have the feeling that Babe will run in any minute to suit up and go hit another home run.

Enter the National Baseball Hall of Fame and Museum — its full name — and be transported into a baseball fantasyland. Straight ahead you'll spot life-size wooden statues of Babe Ruth and Ted Williams. They look so real you can see whisker stubs sprouting from Babe's face as he stares back at you.

In the Cooperstown Room you'll see the evolution of baseball, including a photo of the first Hall of Famers and the $5 Abner Doubleday Baseball that Stephen Clark bought from Abner Graves's family.

The entrance to the Ballparks Room in the Baseball Hall of Fame shows World Series posters. Inside are turnstiles, lockers, dugout benches, and grandstand seats — relics of ballparks of the past.

In the Sports Gallery, zero in on the stats of your favorite Hall of Famer. On the computer you can punch up Roy Campanella's lifetime batting average or find out how many bases Lou Brock stole or how many Gold Gloves Johnny Bench won.

Climb to the second floor and see the old-time baseball uniforms. Check out the baggy, knee-length pants, flannel shirts, and straw caps worn by some of the first organized baseball teams.

On the third floor are **dugout** benches, grandstand seats, turnstiles, and cornerstones from Ebbets Field, Forbes Field, Crosley Field, and the Polo Grounds. None of these parks exist any longer — they all are history.

Smell the memories of leather, dust, and sweat while you stroll by lockers that once belonged to Joe DiMaggio, Stan Musial, and Hank Aaron, who broke Babe Ruth's 714 home run record. The lockers stand side by side, like an all-star baseball team for all time.

Walking through the Hall of Fame, you'll see how much the game has changed over the years. In 1845 Alexander Cartwright, a bank clerk, served on the Knickerbocker Rules Committee, a group formed to set up baseball rules. The commission took the old Town Ball rules and changed them to fit the evolving game of baseball. The new rules became known as the Knickerbocker Rules. Today baseball is still based on the original Knickerbocker Rules.

One rule was to set 42 paces between home and second base, and first and third. This distance gave both teams an even chance, because it takes a batter about four seconds to run from home to first. And a fielder can pick up a ball and throw it to a base in almost the same time. Today there are 90 feet between bases (first and second, second and third).

The Knickerbocker Rules also reduced the original 11 players to 9. And the rules eliminated one catcher and one short fielder and changed the name short fielder to shortstop. Then they adopted from Town Ball the rule of three outs per inning and a nonchangeable batting order. The 21-run game of the Knickerbockers was changed to 9 innings.

Until 1845 there were no true **foul lines** as we know them today. Balls were considered out-of-bounds if hit into areas where there were obstacles, such as buildings or trees. The Knickerbocker Rules said a ball hit outside first or third base was a **foul ball**.

In early baseball the batter stood in his own area, called a batters' area, not on a base. The batter had to run around only three bases to get a run. He didn't have to run back to where he'd hit the ball to get the run. The Knickerbocker Rules put a base at the batters' area. To make a run, the batter had to come back to where he'd hit the ball. Later this batters' base was changed to an iron plate. That's why today home is called **home plate**.

In Town Ball there were no basemen. So when a batter hit the ball, the fielders threw it at the batter to put him out. The batter had to dodge the ball while running the bases. The Knickerbocker Rules outlawed the Town Ball rule of throwing a ball at a runner to put him out. But people who played other forms of baseball kept up the practice for another 15 years.

Pitchers didn't always throw overhand. Until 1884 they had to throw underhand, like pitching pennies or horseshoes. That's why the player who throws the ball to a batter is called a pitcher. Then in 1884 the National Baseball Association voted to allow pitchers to throw the ball with any motion. Most pitchers changed to the overhand pitch, because they could throw the ball faster and more accurately.

Also until 1884 a batter could tell the pitcher what kind of ball he wanted. If the batter asked for a high ball, the **umpire** told the pitcher to throw between the batter's waist and shoulders. If the batter wanted a low ball, the umpire told the pitcher to throw between the batter's waist and at least 1 foot above the ground. If the pitcher threw nine balls without hitting the right spot, the batter walked.

The uniforms, rules, and equipment changed over the years. Take a peek at the Hall of Fame display of baseballs, bats, and gloves. In 1858 the ball weighed 6-1/4 ounces and was 10-1/4 inches around. A modern baseball weighs 5 to 5-1/4 ounces and is 9 to 9-1/4 inches around. Today the smaller size makes it harder for batters to hit one over the fence.

Today's players are luckier than the old-timers. Until 1875 no gloves or other kinds of protection were used. Some catchers wore a rubber mouthpiece to protect their teeth. But most catchers thought fans would call them sissies if they wore mouthpieces. So some catchers lost a few teeth before they retired. A few ended up toothless. Then in 1875 Fred Thayer made the first catcher's mask.

Macho thinking also kept players from using gloves. But that same

A display at the Baseball Hall of Fame shows how catchers' equipment has changed through the years. Inset: *Pitcher Sandy Koufax of the Brooklyn Dodgers shows his game-winning form.*

year Charles C. Waitt had so many bruises on his hands, he wore a glove. He was so ashamed that he used a light-colored one, hoping nobody would spot it. Albert G. Spalding, however, wasn't ashamed to wear a glove. In fact, in 1877 he chose a black glove everyone could see. It was skintight, with the fingertips cut out so he could get a better grip on the ball.

An accident in 1883 launched the modern baseball glove. And that happened only after Arthur Irwin, who played shortstop for a Rhode Island team, broke the third and fourth fingers on his left hand. There were no extra players, so he had to catch with broken fingers.

To protect Irwin's fingers, a glove maker put padding in an oversized driving glove and cut an opening in the back so the hand wouldn't sweat. Then the glove was sewn so the bandaged fingers would fit into one finger hole. Because Irwin didn't flinch from the ball when it came at him, he played better. When other players saw how well Irwin played, they ordered gloves, too. Fans didn't call the players sissies, and gloves became standard equipment.

More macho thinking kept Philadelphia Phillies catcher Red Dooin from being known as the first catcher to wear shin guards and a chest protector. He was so afraid fans would laugh at him that he hid the gear under his uniform for two years. He admitted hiding his gear after New York Giants catcher Roger Bresnahan wore shin guards and a chest protector on the outside of his uniform. Bresnahan also started using a batting helmet after he got beaned by a ball.

And speaking of balls, today about 40 to 50 balls are used in every game. But in the old days teams were lucky to have 2 or 3. By the seventh inning the balls had been batted into lopsided shapes, making them hard to hit. If a ball went into the stands, an official offered the spectator who caught it a free pass to another game if the fan would give the ball back. The official usually got it. No ball, no game. Then in 1916 the owner of the Chicago Cubs, Charles Weeghman, decided to let the fans keep the balls, and other clubs followed suit. By the 1920s it was the custom to let fans keep the balls.

Up to the year 1888, bats were round and could be any length the batter wanted. For the bunt, players used flat-sided bats to keep the ball in the infield. Flat bats were outlawed in 1893.

On a visit to the Hall of Fame you'll even see historic baseball cards, one of the most popular exhibits in the Hall. Some of these cards are worth a lot of money. One is the John Peter "Honus" Wagner T-206 tobacco card. Soon after it was printed, the card was taken off the market because Wagner was upset that he hadn't gotten paid for having his picture on the card.

Since the card was taken off the market before many were sold, the Wagner T-206 became very valuable. In 1991 the hockey player Wayne Gretsky and Los Angeles Kings owner Bruce McNall bought one at auction for $410,000, plus 10 percent commission, for a total of almost half a million dollars.

In the Hall of Fame there are also displays about the minor leagues, youth baseball, postage stamps, and baseball music. With so many exhibits to choose from, you could spend days in the Hall and never get bored.

Satchel Paige warms up before pitching for the Cleveland Indians in an exhibition game against the Chicago Cubs on March 24, 1949.

Chapter Three

For It's Root, Root, Root for the Home Team: The Barriers Come Down

On August 28, 1945, in Brooklyn, New York, a 26-year-old black athlete sat across the desk from Wesley "Branch" Rickey, president of the National League Brooklyn Dodgers. The athlete thought Rickey wanted to ask about creating another black baseball team to be called the Brooklyn Brown Dodgers. He was wrong.

There were already many great black baseball teams — in fact, they had their own organization, the Negro Leagues. In the 1880s Moses and Weldy Walker, two brothers who played for Toledo in the American Association, were the most well-known black players. But what Rickey wanted was to put the first black player on a modern **major league** team. He'd scouted the country for the right player, and some of the names on his list included Satchel Paige, Josh Gibson, James T. "Cool Papa" Bell, and Monte Irvin.

Rickey said that if the athlete proved himself in the Dodger farm club next season, he might move up to the Brooklyn Dodgers. Rickey warned the athlete that if he joined the majors, other clubs, fans, and even his own teammates would put him down. Many wouldn't talk to him. Was he brave enough to take the insults and not lose his cool or quit? Yes he was.

The man was Jack Roosevelt Robinson, and his answer changed baseball history. Robinson was a former University of California football, basketball, and track star. At the time he met Rickey, he was a shortstop for the Negro Leagues' Kansas City Monarchs.

There never was a written law barring blacks from the major leagues. But discrimination had always been the unwritten law. Every player, coach, manager, and sportswriter was white. Negro League players resented being shut out of the major leagues. William "Judy" Johnson, a consistent .300 hitter, said, "The Negro teams are Triple A quality and we can beat any of the white major leagues any day."

Black players made very little money. Sometimes the only money they made was from passing the hat to fans. Traveling for 12 hours at a stretch, they rode in broken-down buses crowded with players. Teams stayed in rooming houses "for Negroes only," two or three to a bed. They spread newspapers on the mattresses to protect themselves from bedbugs and the cold.

In some towns there were no black rooming houses. Cool Papa Bell described the way they lived: "We went into a lot of small towns where they'd never seen a colored person. So we'd pull off the side of the road to sleep. Then we'd go into the next town, hoping we'd find a restaurant willing to serve colored people."

April 15, 1947, was a history-making day. That day Jackie Robinson became the first black player in the major leagues since 1884. He played first base for the Brooklyn Dodgers at Ebbets Field. Protests erupted everywhere. Four Dodgers asked to be traded. Some St. Louis Cardinals threatened to strike.

Ford Frick, president of the National League, said, "I don't care if half the league strikes. Those who do will be suspended and I don't care if it wrecks the National League . . . . This is the United States of America and one citizen has as much right to play as another." His threat worked. Jackie Robinson played all season and won the National League's Rookie of the Year Award.

The first black to play for the American League was Larry Doby. Bill Veeck, owner of the Cleveland Indians, signed him up, and then in 1948 signed the oldest black rookie, 42-year-old Satchel Paige. Roy Campanella came up with the Dodgers in 1948, Willie Mays with the New York Giants in 1951, and Elston Howard with the Yankees in 1955.

Jackie Robinson, right, waits for his turn at bat with Brooklyn Dodgers teammates, from left, Johnny Jorgensen, Pee Wee Reese, and Eddie Stanky.

Women played in the All-American Girls Professional Baseball League from 1943 to 1954. Mementos from that era are displayed in the Women in Baseball exhibit at the Hall of Fame.

By 1959 every major league team had at least one black player. But prejudice didn't stop. While fans cheered black players on the field, off the field they still couldn't eat in the same restaurants or stay in the same hotels as white players. Not until civil rights legislation was passed in the 1960s did black players legally have the same rights as whites. The Baseball Hall of Fame has exhibits showing the changes from discrimination to integration.

Another historic exhibit in the Baseball Hall of Fame, opened in 1988, shows how the "no-women barrier" tumbled down. Called the Women in Baseball exhibit, it honors the 550 women from the United States, Cuba, and Canada who played in the All-American Girls Professional Baseball League (AAGPBL), from 1943 to 1954.

The players of the AAGPBL, the only women's professional baseball league the United States ever had, belonged to teams whose names today would be considered sexist — Peaches, Lassies, and Chicks. Sportswriters called them the Queens of Swat and the Belles of the Ball Game. But they called one another Moe, Nickie, Pepper, and Flash.

The women's league began during World War II. So many men were on the battlefields instead of on the baseball fields that Philip K. Wrigley, owner of the Chicago Cubs, thought the game might die out. So he put together a professional women's league to replace the men's teams.

In May 1943 more than 100 of the best women softball players crowded Chicago's Wrigley Field for tryouts. Most of them were barely out of high school and had never been away from home. Wrigley picked the 60 best players and divided them into four teams. Their 108-game season lasted three months. Players were paid about $125 a week for 6 games and a doubleheader on Sunday. The winner of the first half of the season played the winner of the second half in the Championship Series.

Wrigley wanted his "girls" to play hard baseball but look soft. He insisted they wear short skirts so their shapely legs would attract sellout crowds. The women wanted to wear the same kind of uniform the men wore. But Wrigley insisted on the short skirts. So his players spent a lot of time bandaging cuts they got from sliding into bases.

A shortstop and catcher for three teams, Lavone "Pepper" Davis, said, "It wasn't easy walking around in high heels with a book on your head when you had pulled leg muscles from playing ball all day." To keep their hands soft and fingernails polished, the women were told to scratch a bar of soap before each game. This would also keep dirt from getting under their nails.

Wrigley insisted that his "girls" go to charm school. There they learned how to put on makeup, get in and out of cars without letting their dresses ride above their knees, speak correctly, and flatter a date. But while Wrigley wanted his players to know how to flatter men, he didn't want them to flatter their dates while they were alone with them. So he hired chaperones to go everywhere with his "girls."

Everywhere meant dance clubs, movies, or a walk in the park. Chaperones stuck to the women like glue, even while they were on the playing field. During a close game Shirley Jameson's chaperone actually yanked her off the plate because she wasn't wearing lipstick.

But even with their ladylike manners, the women played hardball. After watching shortstop Dorothy Schroeder work out, the Chicago Cubs manager, Charlie Grimm, said, "If she was a boy, I'd give $50,000 for her."

The All-American Girls Professional Baseball League grew so popular that fan clubs formed. Members followed the women from town to town the way rock star groupies do today. Men fighting overseas sent them marriage proposals. The league went on to include ten teams with more than a million fans a season.

Wrigley sold his interest in the AAGPBL in 1944 when he realized World War II wasn't going to close down the major leagues after all. Franchises ran the women's league until 1954. That's when people lost interest and the AAGPBL struck out forever. In 1992 interest in the league was renewed when *A League of Their Own*, a movie about the AAGPBL, was released. One of the athletes was played by Madonna.

No women have been elected yet to the Baseball Hall of Fame. But the list of members does include top Negro League players, as well as pioneers and executives, umpires, and managers who have made outstanding contributions to the game.

Chapter Four

One, Two, Three Strikes You're Out:
Ridiculous Rules and Incredible Home Runs

Through the years some baseball games sprouted rules that stuck, while others bit the dust. In the 1880s and early 1900s, for example, it was against the law to play baseball on Sunday. If the police spotted a game, they arrested the players.

At an 1891 Sunday game in Cincinnati, fans were told to save their tickets for a refund if police stopped the game. Sure enough, the cops came and carted the team off to jail. Each player had to post a $300 bond to get out. But jail didn't stop players in Ohio. They went across the state line to Kentucky, where Sunday baseball was legal. Eventually, other states and cities legalized Sunday baseball—New York State in 1919, Boston in 1929, and the last holdouts, Pittsburgh and Philadelphia, in the early 1930s.

In the old days not only was the rule "Never on Sunday," but it was also "No Women Allowed at Games." Men thought the foul language, brawls in the stands, and fighting on the field were too uncivilized for women. But women insisted they be allowed to see America's favorite pastime. So in 1867 the New York Knickerbockers declared a special day each month for women and called it Ladies Day.

Men complained that having women at games took away their constitutional right to swear and spit. But some owners didn't mind having women at games. To protect women's delicate ears, owners set aside special

A Baseball Hall of Fame exhibit features a collection of bats and balls used by baseball heroes of the past and present. Inset: *Boston Red Sox champion Ted Williams shows how to use a bat.*

walkways for women to get to their seats without having to pass by the swearing and spitting men. To make the women comfortable, some owners brought in long cushioned seats with high backs, called settees.

Over the years private walkways and settees disappeared. But not until the 1970s did the tradition of Ladies Day end. It wasn't because women stopped coming to games — it was because so many did come. Owners realized they could charge women full price instead of half price, which was the cost on Ladies Day. Women grumbled, but they shelled out the extra money.

While it took 90 years to end Ladies Day, other traditions started on the spur of the moment. On opening day in 1910, on a whim, American League umpire Billy Evans strolled to President William Howard Taft's box and asked him if he wanted to toss out the first ball. Taft jumped at the chance. And ever since it has been the tradition for presidents of the United States to throw out the first ball of the season.

Another tradition was started in the 1940s by a man who was a team manager for only three games. Luke Sewell, manager of the Cincinnati Reds, thought if he stopped the action on the field at some point in the game, fans would get bored and go buy food and drinks. So he told the grounds keepers to bore the fans by cleaning up the infield after the fifth inning. Sewell's idea worked. Fans swarmed the refreshment stands, and the tradition of dragging the infield during the game was born.

The seventh-inning stretch began for health reasons. The chaplain at Manhattan College in New York made his students sit straight and still during baseball games. Then he realized that sitting so rigid could damage their muscles. So to give them a break, he let students stand and stretch during the seventh inning. Baseball coaches picked up on the idea, and the seventh-inning stretch became a tradition.

Crowds at the first modern World Series in 1903, between the Boston Pilgrims (later the Red Sox) and the Pittsburgh Pirates, created a special ground rule. So many people came to the opening game in Pittsburgh that they crashed onto the field. Even horse-mounted police couldn't get them to leave. The outfield was roped off to make room for the overflow fans and to allow the game to go on. And a temporary rule was created — any ball hit into the crowd was an automatic **double**.

There was no World Series in 1904 because New York Giants owner John T. Brush refused to play those "**bush leaguers** from Boston." But after being put down by the American League for his refusal, he allowed the Giants to play the Philadelphia Athletics in 1905.

Jimmy Piersall caused a new permanent rule to be written into the books after he hit his 100th home run on June 23, 1963. Piersall celebrated by running the bases backward. Although fans loved the stunt, club owners didn't. They wrote a rule saying a player must face the bases while running. A player who runs backward is automatically out.

Besides ridiculous rules and traditions, there have been many incredible home run legends. One of the most incredible happened on October 1, 1932, at Chicago's Wrigley Field. It was the third game of the World Series, between the New York Yankees and the Chicago Cubs. When George Herman "Babe" Ruth came to bat against Cubs pitcher Charlie Root, the first pitch was a strike. Babe held up his finger. "That's one." The second pitch was a ball. Babe held up two fingers. "That's two." The count rose to two strikes and two balls. Then Babe looked at Root and pointed at the fence. On the next pitch, Babe whacked the ball. It sailed over the fence.

Another baseball legend who hit amazing home runs was New York Yankee first baseman Henry Louis "Lou" Gehrig, called the Iron Horse for his stamina. He played 2,130 consecutive games during his career. He kept playing even when he became ill with amyotrophic lateral sclerosis, a fatal muscular disease now known as Lou Gehrig's disease.

Gehrig was the first 20th-century player to hit four consecutive homers in one game. And when he came to the plate again on that memorable day, he would have hit a fifth. But the ball hit the scoreboard and fell back inside the field. If the ball had gone to the right or left of the scoreboard, it would have gone over the fence. Gehrig was such a respected player that the U.S. Post Office issued a stamp in his honor.

Ed Delahanty, outfielder for the Philadelphia Phillies, also had his unbelievable home run day. On July 13, 1896, he slugged home runs to left, right, and center fields. Then he hit another homer inside the park. His teammates swallowed him up. Fans went crazy. No one wanted the day to end. But the great thing about baseball is that it never ends. There's always another inning, another game, another season.

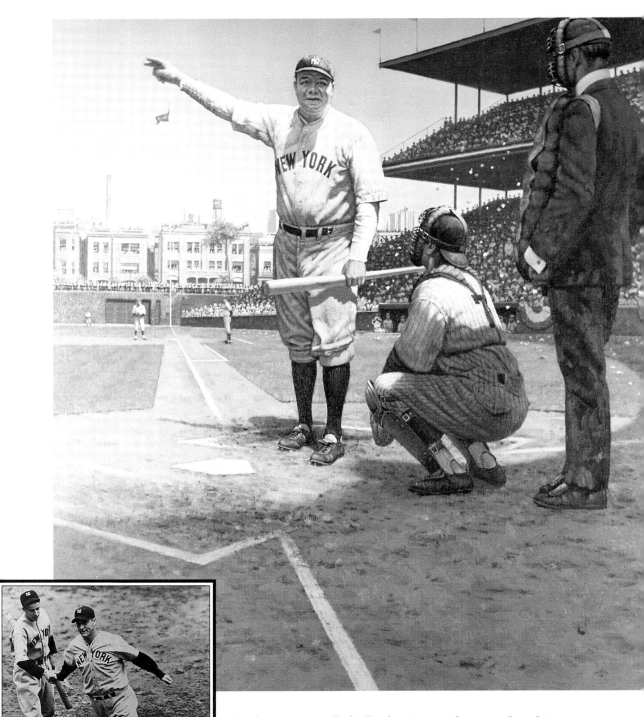

In this painting, Babe Ruth points to the spot where his home run ball will hit during the third game of the World Series in 1932. Inset: Lou Gehrig runs the bases after hitting a home run for the New York Yankees.

Mickey Mantle gets ready to take a swing during an Annual Hall of Fame Game at Doubleday Field outside the Baseball Hall of Fame.

Chapter Five

At the Old Ball Game:
Hall of Fame Day and Its Mighty Players

It's something like going to heaven. — Charlie Gehringer

Changes your life. For the rest of my life I'll be known as Hall of Famer George Kell. And 100 years from now, my great-grandchildren will come here and they'll think I was as good as Cobb or Ruth. — George Kell

Each year in July or August, over 10,000 baseball fans from all over the world flock to Cooperstown for Hall of Fame Day. At induction ceremonies for new members, honorees receive a photo of the bronze plaque that hangs in the Hall of Fame in their honor, and a specially designed ring.

Afterward there's an autograph session for fans to get signatures from their favorite players. Then one team from the National League and one team from the American League play in the Annual Hall of Fame Game at Doubleday Field. Fans cheer and wonder which of the players they're watching will someday be Hall of Famers themselves.

The odds are against them. Fewer than 1 percent of the over 10,000 people who have played in the major leagues have been elected. If your favorite player isn't in the Hall of Fame, you can probably blame the Baseball Writers Association of America (BBWAA). This organization decides who gets in. Sometimes they're way off base. Eleven of the sportswriters didn't vote for Babe Ruth in the first election, in 1936!

This is the way the election works. A screening committee picks 30 names to put on the ballot. Members of the BBWAA vote for up to 10 nominees. Candidates who receive 75 percent of the ballots are elected. To be eligible, players must have been in the major leagues for at least ten years. But they must have been retired from the majors for five years before election day.

Besides the players elected by ballot, a veterans committee may elect two people from the categories of managers, umpires, pioneers and executives, and Negro Leaguers. The latter must have played for at least ten years in the Negro Leagues before 1946. Or they can be voted in if their years in the Negro Leagues and their years in the major leagues add up to ten. To be elected, players need more than talent. They must show integrity, sportsmanship, and character. However, some players have been elected who didn't show these qualities.

Probably the Hall of Famer who showed the least sportsmanship, integrity, and character was Tyrus R. "Ty" Cobb. Many consider him baseball's greatest player, and sportswriter Jimmy Cannon of the *New York Post* called him "the greatest piece of baseball machinery that ever stepped on a diamond."

In 1905, at age 18, Cobb began his baseball career with the Detroit Tigers. He had a reputation for playing dirty, especially for using his hand-sharpened spikes to ram into basemen's legs. During one of his attacks, he raced toward third baseman Ossie Bluege of the Washington Senators. Recalled Bluege: "Cobb didn't slide. He took off and came at me in midair, spikes first, about 4 or 5 feet off the ground, so help me just like a rocket."

Cobb's spikes sank into Bluege's arm, cutting his skin. Bluege was so mad he tried to hit Cobb with the ball. But the umpire pulled Bluege off and threw Cobb out of the game. After that, even the kindhearted Philadelphia Athletics manager, Cornelius A. "Connie" Mack, called Ty Cobb "the dirtiest player the game has ever known."

Cobb's teammates got back at him for being so mean. They sawed his bats in half, ripped his uniform, and locked him in hotel bathrooms. His teammates weren't the only ones who got back at him. His opponents did too. In the 1909 World Series, Cobb, the batting champion of the American League, faced Honus Wagner, batting champion of the National League.

Wagner was playing second base when Cobb charged toward him, aiming his spikes at Wagner's shins. Wagner tagged Cobb out by smashing the ball across his mouth. Nevertheless, those two heroes, who acted like kids on a sandlot, were among the first players elected into the Hall of Fame.

Other players did unfair things that cut them out of the running completely. The most notorious of these athletes were eight members of the Chicago White Sox who played in the 1919 World Series against the Cincinnati Reds. The cheating White Sox players, who soon came to be called the "Black" Sox, were Eddie Cicotte, Claude "Lefty" Williams, Happy Felsch, Chick Gandil, Buck Weaver, Swede Risberg, Fred McMullin, and "Shoeless" Joe Jackson, the only rookie ever to hit .400.

In 1919, teams played a best-of-nine World Series. In the opening game White Sox pitcher Eddie Cicotte's second pitch hit a Cincinnati batter. Honest catcher Ray Schalk thought Cicotte wasn't paying attention to signals. But gamblers knew that the pitch meant the fix was on.

The second game was a cheating replay. Then in the third game, Dickie Kerr, a Chicago player who kept his Sox clean, pitched a shutout against the Reds. When the Sox lost the fourth and fifth games, rumors popped up that Chicago was throwing the Series. To stop the rumors, the "Black" Sox decided to play to win in the sixth and seventh games. And they did. The gamblers weren't happy. They warned the "Black" Sox that their families would be in danger if they won the Series. Scared by these threats, the Sox lost the eighth game and the Series.

White Sox owner Charles Comiskey learned that the Series had been fixed. He created an investigating committee headed by Judge Kenesaw Mountain Landis, who soon became baseball's first commissioner. Enough evidence was found to bring the eight cheaters to trial. Although the evidence pointed to a guilty verdict, the jury found them innocent. But they didn't get off without punishment. Judge Landis banned the notorious eight from major league baseball for life.

Throwing games wasn't the only kind of cheating that kept dishonest players out of the Hall of Fame. In 1898 the Philadelphia Phillies invented their own dirty trick. Cincinnati Reds third base coach Tommy Corcoran discovered the Phillies' way of cheating. During a game, he kicked up something long and black in the dirt. Corcoran thought it was a snake. But when he jerked it up, yards of cable wire popped out.

He followed the cable across the field into the Phillies' clubhouse. There Corcoran saw Philadelphia catcher Morgan Murphy spying through a peephole with binoculars and tapping a telegraph buzzer. Murphy was reading the catcher's signals and beeping them to the Phillies third base coach, who relayed them to the batter.

While these dirty tricks may make baseball look like a cheater's game, there are many more honest players than dishonest. And they care about the game, and their fans.

One such player was Ted Williams, outfielder for the Boston Red Sox, whose .406 batting average in 1941 has never been beaten. During his 1966 induction speech, Williams said, "It's the greatest thrill of my life. . . . Baseball gives every American boy a chance to excel . . . and I've been a very lucky guy to have worn a baseball uniform."

Ted Williams understood how important it is to fans to get a nod, a smile, or an autograph from a player. In 1987 he was in Cooperstown for the Hall of Fame weekend when he decided to get in some fishing. He walked out of his hotel early in the morning and spotted fans lined up waiting for autographs. Some had been there all night, and Williams didn't want to let them down. So he signed autographs until everybody had one. Then he went to fish.

Babe Ruth was another player who knew how important autographs are to fans. After a game in Pittsburgh, he started signing autographs. He signed and signed. Finally somebody brought him a chair, and Babe sat and signed until everybody there had his autograph.

Sanford "Sandy" Koufax, pitcher for the Los Angeles Dodgers, also respected the game and his fans. During the 1963 World Series, between the Yankees and the Dodgers, Koufax didn't want to let down his fans or his team. But his elbow was in severe pain from arthritis. So before each

The Chicago White Sox team of 1919 poses for a photograph during the World Series games against the Cincinnati Reds. Eight members of the team were accused of cheating in the "Black" Sox scandal.

game he applied massive heat treatments to his elbow to make it flexible. Then after each game he soaked his elbow in ice to keep the swelling down. Despite his pain, he never missed his rotation. He pitched the pennant-clinching game for the Dodgers. Then he helped them win the World Series.

Albert W. Kaline, right fielder for the Detroit Tigers, respected the integrity of baseball so much that he wouldn't take a penny more than he thought he deserved. In 1971, when the Tigers offered him a contract for $100,000, he said, "I don't deserve such a salary. I didn't have a good enough season last year. This ball club has been so fair and decent to me, I'd prefer to have you give it to me when I rate it."

And then there was Chicago White Sox owner Charles Comiskey. He loved the game so much that on a rainy Saturday, while players sat on the bench to keep dry, Comiskey stood in the muddy field with his pants legs rolled up. He soaked up water with sponges and wrung them into a pail, trying to get the diamond in shape to play.

Mementos from these baseball players, managers, and owners are on display in the Baseball Hall of Fame. You'll see Lou Brock's running shoes, Mickey Mantle's Number 7 uniform shirts, and souvenirs from the most famous infield trio: Joe Tinker's shoes, Johnny Evers's glove, and Frank Chance's bat.

There are more than 6,000 artifacts on display in the Baseball Hall of Fame. And they all echo with the cheers of a thousand days of baseball dreams.

National Baseball
Hall of Fame Members

Cooperstown, New York

Electees to the Hall of Fame

Aaron, Henry L. 1982
*Alexander, Grover C. 1938
*Alston, Walter E. 1983
*Anson, Adrian C. "Cap" 1939
Aparicio, Luis E. 1984
*Appling, Lucius B. "Luke" 1964
*Averill, H. Earl 1975
*Baker, J. Franklin 1955
*Bancroft, David J. 1971
Banks, Ernest 1977
Barlick, Albert J. 1989
*Barrow, Edward G. 1953
*Beckley, Jacob P. 1971
*Bell, James T. "Cool Papa" 1974
Bench, Johnny L. 1989
*Bender, Charles A. "Chief" 1953
Berra, Lawrence P. "Yogi" 1972
*Bottomley, James L. 1974
Boudreau, Louis 1970
*Bresnahan, Roger P. 1945
Brock, Louis C. 1985
*Brouthers, Dennis "Dan" 1945
*Brown, Mordecai P. 1949
*Bulkeley, Morgan G. 1937
*Burkett, Jesse C. 1946
*Campanella, Roy 1969
Carew, Rodney C. 1991
*Carey, Max G. 1961
*Cartwright, Alexander J., Jr. 1938
*Chadwick, Henry 1938
*Chance, Frank L. 1946
*Chandler, Albert B. "Happy" 1982
*Charleston, Oscar M. 1976

*Chesbro, John D. 1946
*Clarke, Frederick C. 1945
*Clarkson, John G. 1963
*Clemente, Roberto W. 1973
*Cobb, Tyrus R. 1936
*Cochrane, Gordon S. "Mickey" 1947
*Collins, Edward T. 1939
*Collins, James J. 1945
*Combs, Earle B. 1970
*Comiskey, Charles A. 1939
*Conlan, John B. "Jocko" 1974
*Connolly, Thomas H. 1953
*Connor, Roger 1976
*Coveleski, Stanley A. 1969
*Crawford, Samuel E. 1957
*Cronin, Joseph H. 1956
*Cummings, William A. "Candy" 1939
*Cuyler, Hazen S. "Kiki" 1968
Dandridge, Raymond E. 1987
*Dean, Jay H. "Dizzy" 1953
*Delahanty, Edward J. 1945
Dickey, William M. 1954
*Dihigo, Martin 1977
DiMaggio, Joseph P. 1955
Doerr, Robert N. P. 1986
*Drysdale, Donald S. 1984
*Duffy, Hugh 1945
Evans, William G. 1973
*Evers, John J. 1946
*Ewing, William B. "Buck" 1939
*Faber, Urban C. "Red" 1964
Feller, Robert W. A. 1962

With a wave of his cap, Reggie Jackson acknowledges the cheers of fans in right field.

Ferrell, Richard B. Ferrell 1984
Fingers, Roland G. 1992
*Flick, Elmer H. 1963
Ford, Edward C. "Whitey" 1974
*Foster, Andrew "Rube" 1981
*Foxx, James E. 1951
*Frick, Ford C. 1970
*Frisch, Frank F. 1947
*Galvin, James F. "Pud" 1965
*Gehrig, H. Louis 1939
*Gehringer, Charles L. 1949
*Gibson, Joshua 1972
Gibson, Robert 1981
*Giles, Warren C. 1979
*Gomez, Vernon L. "Lefty" 1972
*Goslin, Leon A. "Goose" 1968
*Greenberg, Henry B. 1956
*Griffith, Clark C. 1946
*Grimes, Burleigh A. 1964
*Grove, Robert M. "Lefty" 1947
*Hafey, Charles J. "Chick" 1971
*Haines, Jesse J. "Pop" 1970
Hamilton, William R. 1961
*Harridge, William 1972
*Harris, Stanley R. "Bucky" 1975
*Hartnett, Charles L. "Gabby" 1955
*Heilmann, Harry E. 1952
Herman, William J. 1975
*Hooper, Harry B. 1971
*Hornsby, Rogers 1942
*Hoyt, Waite C. 1969
*Hubbard, R. Cal 1976
*Hubbell, Carl O. 1947
*Huggins, Miller J. 1964
Hunter, James A. "Catfish" 1987

Irvin, Monford "Monte" 1973
Jackson, Reggie 1993
*Jackson, Travis C. "Stonewall"
   1982
Jenkins, Ferguson A. 1991
*Jennings, Hugh A. 1945
*Johnson, Byron B. "Ban" 1937
*Johnson, Walter P. 1936
*Johnson, William J. "Judy" 1975
*Joss, Adrian 1978
Kaline, Albert W. 1980
*Keefe, Timothy J. 1964
*Keeler, William H. "Willie" 1939
Kell, George C. 1983
*Kelley, Joseph J. 1971
*Kelly, George L. 1973
*Kelly, Michael J. "King" 1945
Killebrew, Harmon C. 1984
Kiner, Ralph M. 1975
*Klein, Charles H. 1980
*Klem, William L. 1953
Koufax, Sanford 1972
*Lajoie, Napoleon "Larry" 1937
*Landis, Kenesaw M. 1944
*Lazzeri, Anthony M. 1991
Lemon, Robert G. 1976
Leonard, Walter F. "Buck" 1972
*Lindstrom, Frederick C. 1976
*Lloyd, John H. 1977
*Lombardi, Ernest 1986
Lopez, Alfonso R. 1977
*Lyons, Theodore A. 1955
*Mack, Cornelius A. "Connie" 1937
*MacPhail, Leland S. "Larry" 1978
Mantle, Mickey C. 1974

*Manush, Henry E. "Heinie" 1964
*Maranville, Walter J. "Rabbit" 1954
Marichal, Juan A. 1983
*Marquard, Richard W. "Rube" 1971
Mathews, Edwin L. 1978
*Mathewson, Christopher 1936
Mays, Willie H. 1979
*McCarthy, Joseph V. 1957
*McCarthy, Thomas F. 1946
McCovey, Willie L. "Stretch" 1986
*McGinnity, Joseph J. 1946
*McGowan, William A. 1992
*McGraw, John J. 1937
*McKechnie, William B. 1962
*Medwick, Joseph A. 1968
Mize, John R. 1981
Morgan, Joe L. 1990
Musial, Stanley F. 1969
Newhouser, Harold 1992
*Nichols, Charles A. "Kid" 1949
*O'Rourke, James H. 1945
*Ott, Melvin T. 1951
*Paige, Leroy R. "Satchel" 1971
Palmer, James A. 1990
*Pennock, Herbert J. 1948
Perry, Gaylord J. 1991
*Plank, Edward S. 1946
*Radbourne, Charles G. 1939
Reese, Harold H. "Pee Wee" 1984
*Rice, Edgar C. "Sam" 1963
*Rickey, W. Branch 1967
*Rixey, Eppa 1963
Roberts, Robin E. 1976
Robinson, Brooks C., Jr. 1983
Robinson, Frank 1982

*Robinson, Jack R. 1962
*Robinson, Wilbert 1945
*Roush, Edd J. 1962
*Ruffing, Charles H. "Red" 1967
*Rusie, Amos W. 1977
*Ruth, George "Babe" 1936
*Schalk, Raymond W. 1955
Schoendienst, Albert F. "Red" 1989
Seaver, George T. 1992
*Sewell, Joseph W. 1977
*Simmons, Aloysius H. 1953
*Sisler, George H. 1939
Slaughter, Enos B. "Country" 1985
Snider, Edwin D. "Duke" 1980
Spahn, Warren E. 1973
*Spalding, Albert G. 1939
*Speaker, Tristram E. 1937
Stargell, Wilver D. "Willie" 1988
*Stengel, Charles D. "Casey" 1966
*Terry, William H. 1954
*Thompson, Samuel L. 1974
*Tinker, Joseph B. 1946
*Traynor, Harold J. "Pie" 1948
*Vance, Arthur C. "Dazzy" 1955
*Vaughan, Joseph F. "Arky" 1985
*Veeck, Bill 1991
*Waddell, George E. "Rube" 1946
Wagner, John P. "Honus" 1936
*Wallace, Roderick J. "Bobby" 1953
*Walsh, Edward A. 1946
*Waner, Lloyd J. 1967
*Waner, Paul G. 1952
*Ward, John M. 1964
*Weiss, George M. 1971
*Welch, Michael F. 1973

*Wheat, Zachariah D. 1959
Wilhelm, James Hoyt 1985
Williams, Billy L. 1987
Williams, Theodore S. 1966
*Wilson, Lewis R. "Hack" 1979
*Wright, George 1937
*Wright, William H. "Harry" 1953
Wynn, Early 1972
Yastrzemski, Carl M. "Yaz" 1989
*Yawkey, Thomas A. 1980
*Young, Denton T. "Cy" 1937
*Youngs, Ross M. 1972

*Deceased

Glossary

batting average A measure of a batter's success at the plate. Batting averages are figured by dividing the number of hits by the times at bat.

bush leaguer An inferior player.

diamond The infield; also the baseball playing field.

double A two-base hit.

dugout The place where a team sits, usually on benches, while waiting to bat or play the field.

foul ball A ball hit outside the foul lines.

foul line Either of two straight lines going from the rear corner of home plate through the corners of first and third bases, and straight out to the end of the baseball field. The foul line indicates the area in which a fair ball can be hit.

home plate The place where the hitter stands at bat.

home run A hit that allows the batter to run around all the bases and score a run.

major leagues The highest-ranked teams in organized baseball. Major league teams are divided into the American League and the National League.

umpire The person who rules on plays.

World Series The series of games played each fall between the championship teams of baseball's major leagues.

Willie Mays makes a catch during a 1954 World Series game.

Index

Hank Aaron gets ready to take a swing. Aaron holds the home run record for baseball.